THE NATIONAL POETRY SERIES

The National Poetry Series was established in 1978 to ensure the publication of five poetry books annually through participating publishers. Publication is funded by the Lannan Foundation; the late James A. Michener and Edward J. Piszek through the Copernicus Society of America; Stephen Graham; International Institute of Modern Letters; Joyce & Seward Johnson Foundation; Juliet Lea Hillman Simonds Foundation; and, the Tiny Tiger Foundation. This project also is supported in part by an award from the National Endowment for the Arts, which believes that a great nation deserves grea

2004 COMPETITION WINNERS

David Friedman of New York, New York, *The Welcome*
Chosen by Stephen Dunn,
University of Illinois Press

Tyehimba Jess of Brooklyn, New York, *Leadbelly*
Chosen by Brigit Pegeen Kelly,
Verse Press

Corinne Lee of Austin, Texas, *PYX*
Chosen by Pattiann Rogers,
Penguin Books

Ange Mlinko of Brooklyn, New York, *Starred Wire*
Chosen by Bob Holman,
Coffee House Press

Camille Norton of Stockton, California, *Corruption*
Chosen by Campbell McGrath,
HarperCollins

STARRED WIRE

Starred Wire

poems by

ANGE MLINKO

COFFEE HOUSE PRESS

COVER & BOOK DESIGN Linda S. Koutsky
COVER PAINTING © Josh Dorman
AUTHOR PHOTOGRAPH © Samir S. Patel

Coffee House Press books are available to the trade through our primary distributor, Consortium Book Sales & Distribution, 1045 Westgate Drive, Saint Paul, MN 55114. For personal orders, catalogs, or other information, write to: Coffee House Press, 27 North Fourth Street, Suite 400, Minneapolis, MN 55401.

Coffee House Press is a nonprofit literary publishing house. Support from private foundations, corporate giving programs, government programs, and generous individuals help make the publication of our books possible. We gratefully acknowledge their support in detail in the back of this book.

Good books are brewing at coffeehousepress.org

LIBRARY OF CONGRESS CATALOGING-IN-PUBLICATION DATA
Mlinko, Ange.
Starred wire / by Ange Mlinko.
p. cm.
ISBN-13: 978-1-56689-177-6 (alk. paper)
ISBN-10: 1-56689-177-9 (alk. paper)
I. Title.
PS3563.L58S73 2005
811'.54—dc22
2005012568

FIRST EDITION | FIRST PRINTING
1 3 5 7 9 8 6 4 2
Printed in the United States

Some of these poems have appeared or are forthcoming in the following magazines:

Aufgabe, The Butcher Shop, Canwehaveourballback.com, Combo, Conjunctions, Fulcrum, The Germ, The Hat, Insurance, Jacket, The Poetry Project Newsletter, The Poker, Pressed Wafer, Sal Mimeo, Rattapallax, Veritas, The World, and *Xantippe.*

"The Docent of Evening" was published as a broadside by the Center for Book Arts in New York City.

A million thanks to these editors, to Bob Holman, and to my husband Steven.

CONTENTS

for my parents, Sandor and Elena Mlinko;
and my son, Jake McNamara

. . . now I must wait for her to speak
The meanings I must negate before
I am admitted to the gayest person.

—DAVID SCHUBERT

LÀ

Perhaps one wishes in Lisbon to be taken for a Brazilian
& have one's picture taken by a gaggle of boys
who express admiration yet desist from molestation
or maybe you know Lisbon to be the place where peace is purchased
at the price of regular shop hours, so up winding paths with lilacs
different from the kind you're used to flippered over gates
giving off amazing scents that pierce you so in the first breath
you can't capture them again in succeeding ones; then,
then you think You're In Lisbon; or not until
you sit down for dinner and see twenty combinations of salt cod & potato
when a slim very black man from Mozambique strikes up
a conversation do you think you're not in Lisbon? In Lisbon
there's an Arab quarter; it borders on the Castelo
whose blue peacocks and white, white swans and black, tend lilies.
While looking at the Tagus, you could swear you were in Lisbon.
Descending through the Arab quarter, you could swear
you were in Fès. In the Fès medina you could swear you were
in a desert Venice. Venice must be like Boston, on the water
north of things' center, self-sufficient like an athenaeum.
So maybe Lisbon's like Philadelphia, losing all its stars
to New York, in its case Paris? In Philadelphia you sometimes
think you're in Boston, and vice versa; now I'd throw in
Brooklyn too. I doubt this happens in Fès. Fès has orange trees.

In a dream grief feels like grief, joy feels like joy,
adrenaline in any case is adrenaline surging through the veins.
Why do dreams affect us so strongly, turning innocents
into incubi or worse making us fall in love and ruin our lives?

In dreams there is communication between interior and exterior,
as they say of labyrinths. That means there's at least one exit.
But all the gates and ports may be put on alert.
You may get a malady. Your passport might get stolen.
Prepare to dream of Fès. Go to Boston.

IMAGINARY STANDARD DISTANCE

Where the scenery is finer, and life is a thesis

Blue equals blue and lemon equals lemon

Here at my desk or under the umbrella

There where the waiters spread tablecloths

Markless as the sails blooming on the bay

As if one could go from easel to mural

Factoring in more canvas, purer economics,

But not the arms' desire to hold, no

Speaking of the roses grown to obscure the rose-names

Each appears as your personal copy

And Sebastian is Viola's brother

And Viola is Sebastian's sister

And that is all the axiom you get

When the bugle wakes up as sculpture

Solstice enlarging the pupil

Under the logoed umbrellas

I'll have worked out the laws for this

Till my hair turns penciled

KEYS & SCALES

Back when maps were dangerous it was seditious
To give one to a foreigner; feeling so perfectly calligraphic that,
Implying the limp like an iamb superseded what was said of one
By the words themselves, one slyly wrote across the desert,

Allaying the panic took a device to craft a presence.
To say, in search of a role, that a double bend in the river
Was a perimeter of repatriation,
We tried that of believers, like quoted back to itself

The wilderness took shape; the stars were of where
Two had met, in honeydew shadow, and made maps praise.

RIDDEN PILLION

. . . That's the thing: receding loft space, exposed pipes that could pass
for clothes poles stripped of their closets, pressed tin or zinc ceilings
with the futon's pattern reflected there like a suggestion
that maybe the chamber was created by Matissean say-so,
half boudoir half studio, the far end paintings stacked thick
and the near end: opened envelopes, clementine crates,
the vast landslide of a paper trove and double doors flung out
not the honeyed glass of Amsterdam (Museum District)
but an andante you couldn't even play yet it manages
to shoehorn Proust into what's likely a Christmas carol—
What poignancy does the ragged hymen of loose-leaf give
to the kicky triplets coming down the scale to a phone number,
an emigrant butterfly, and the *face in the sun* I'll have nightmares of?

Yellow leaves double light, make me squint like new snow.

Fingerprints on a windowpane: the beginning of painting?

The thing comes down on a jaw of pines and water towers.

It exercises cerise . . .

SECRET CHELSEA

The painting at the heart of evening dries slowly.

The youth risk their evening, the early part of it at least,
in circulating among installations.

The false rich and the false poor exchange their vintage and their
couture; the jokey vouvoyant in the antechambers of "this-isn't-
really-a-jail" to "so-this-is-a-penthouse" delights in misreadings:
after a lifetime of embassies, who's to say there is a world?
Chaperoned into evening

the oils stay youngest longest.

SURELY THE SHAMBLES WILL NOT DESERT THE BANK

If the count's bride is not a blonde?
Is the nightmare just a dream?
Will the painting be returned?
Two night guards encounter levity—
They can only take from the walls what they can run with.
They've been on the inside so long
Risking discovery by radiograph
Of quarantined crates of fleur-de-sel, "Lavender Mist," & tigers.
Gold leaf tonnages.
Between them they have several international languages.
"Beijing is Portuguese for kiss," e.g.
Secret arts acquired in cloven pine prisons.
Stalking techniques.
Submarine instruments—
Woodwinds leak.

The woodwinds say
"I'm taking your painting down to the Devil's Triangle
& there it's gonna stay."

CEREMONY FOR REMOVING A PAINTING

Wake with hands clasped overhead like the bow on a present

Undo the hands and open

Those eyes, themselves beautiful to see

Maintaining the arms in a position of luxuriant openness

Swan over to the wall, the oil, off-rhymed as

Loving a small canvas, which beckons

Like a low voice, means going close

With compatible heights as in waltzing

The head adoringly tilted back

Think of the many times you corrected the tilt

Have an assistant at hand with the tasseled pillow

Have clean hands or better, white gloves

Lift slightly up and out till the ferrule disengages

A bell rings and a light goes on then off, simulating lightning

Tell it it is a lovely painting

About to be schlepped to the Principino on horseback

The secret art of wrapping a canvas can't be repeated

Meanwhile among the mummies one was a dancer

She used to sit beside a throne like the silent Russian letter

That directs the leading consonant to be softer

ROMANCE

Apart from the ligneous Sanskrit lilacs,
there was a strange purplish flower constructed
like a clock bees could not be deterred from
—so engrossed they were, groomed by a finger;
it was the Danish boy who claimed to have had
a hard time learning German, but not English,
what an older man teaches to a Japanese girl
among the fig trees and stone basins,
as much integer as virgin, when the skinheads come
to the southeast staircase by the Greek marbles,
the only published place with a bathroom.
Security caught one of them writing a novel,
Smaragdus. Taking calcined seaweed ashes,
cuttlefish ink, and a young salmon on its way back
to freshwater, it was possible to make an elixir
that would make one a weapon: a full-grown man.
It was embarrassing to be transported
on the howdah when preferring to be peripatetic.
An assignation awaited us.
Someone said Portuguese was a dialect
of Spanish; though we were neither,
without a drop of such blood as sang in the veins
of Camões, the bathroom was faïence,
steam on things, like wax on Fassi writing tablets.
In addition to green, brown, and blue fatigues
there was silver camouflage to wear
in the coastal mists to complete
theological appearances,

unmolding the thoughts we bore the brunt of
in order to exaggerate into paradise
displacing pages toward the shore:
where one was a citizen of every *part*
of paradise before one came to dwell
in its Rome, and call it Literature-by-the-Sea.

ERETHISM

The Idea in its manger: infant incunabulum.
The mind facing a hand outstretched into a star.

Negative hands place the world right at or next to itself,
since the first self-portrait is of the hand itself;

positive hands send vectors of Boolean chastity into delirium.
". . . his charwoman could never finish reading Leonardo's palm."

In the opulence of an Archimedean pinkie
lifted above a pair of tiny scales, is the only world;

from highlight to crosshatch, in the Aeolian distances,
amid such gypsies as one becomes in the true illusion.

FEMME FATALE GEOGRAPHY

1. *Monet Lake*

She hides in the Midwest, tucked behind an ear like a blonde in corn

Between the baby sleeping and the husband studying
She can't play music

Seething like champagne or a midnight city where girls
Cross big avenues alone

She keeps enjoining the children, Be careful of the windmill!

This isn't the same village where a bucket on a rope
Hung on weighted branch
Balanced in the fork of a pole
Brings water to the second floor

Wild birds don't glean from the chickens
That seed can be hulled from her hand

Someone repairs a shutter
Another drags provisions home
Greeted by a small child
Water freezes around the boats
A sort of street fair develops on the river

Man-made Monet Lake's shaped like an eye

But safe within a general surround of Realism

She puts her eyes to the open lozenges of the fence
Glad she is not in Carleton E. Watkins wilderness

Though there is a real man in the center of that Eye

Drowned the winter before, or the winter before that
And he's what the neighbors see everything through

2. *Vertigo Tree*

A Californian dreams it is European
To live in San Francisco, deriding nature

Denying *The Birds* souvenirs
Though the donkeys are good actors
As seen on outdoor screens in summer
At Picnic University

"All the movies are talking about us"
Say the lovers

The fact is nature makes him taller
Amid the hills palms pines

As stools do when it gets to be the rage
To put stools at the horseshoe bar

Because it is European to stroll
Into palm fronds like false whiskers
And the hills which
Like shaving on a ship
Cause beards indirectly

Dreaming his mustache is excessive
At the top of a palm

Dreaming
Like skates at the repeal of skates that all things deuce
Meet bad fates

Adieu, old countree

From the top he can savor milkshake stucco terraces

The blonde wines

"You must be European,"
He thinks at the brunette bob with the latté

He gets a taste for fresh fruit, just fresh fruit
As rings taken off for a massage are forgotten

THE TREASURY OF PLAIN SENSE

My only recourse lay in a sort of divination,
lying down conjuring the Fred and Ginger building

so to pollenate my categories like catbirds and cowbirds.
"Missing footage suggests she lost an arm."

Subtitles appear as grass under our feet
though we would like to read what they say of us

(with the fungible singers of the fainter ochers
droning through the ivy netting on rash brick):

Louis Sullivan's National Farmers Bank
"Designed to look like a treasure chest"

The Women's Auxiliary of the Odd Fellows
"Rebekah carrying water from the Source"

The Morrow Plots, Urbana-Champaign
"Invention of crop rotation"

Daffodils (half asparagus, half bellwether)
tap a yellow chalk dust off their finger-eyes.

THE INTRIGUES

If every page was a frontispiece, and a book not that
laborious farming to some catastrophic end
which copying eyes would retrace, then I could
dispense with jealousy, I mean genealogy,
and be original every time, for the conversions
that inspiration is. A phantom face value haunts me,
but the inverted library; candles at the bottom of the pool;
these are the ghosts of the glass house designed
to be invisible in a wilderness; or I could begin
to incorporate all the reflections of things
that certify their inversions. Meanwhile the music
strobes so rapidly it uncoils in understanding, not time,
adrift in technical registers holding relations in light patterns
all the night till morning's mimosas under blue sky embowering
our nicer noise to a gold-stringed noon acoustic.

A, I do not know if you are negative or intensive,
in a city like a double window whereby all images
of real-life death, like photography a kind of painting
different ways around the park and through it
shadows feint across paths fallen trees.
If it is spiritual having applications to make,
dogs patterning imprimatur, let flowers grow always in defiles
gluing flame to flame in endless spring duplications.
Under the arcade, thinking the landscape
in the mirrored building is the true outside
a sparrow butts its reflections like handwriting
meeting itself on both sides of a diary page.

And not to be trapped in a dream, a journey as far
as the looking glass, which extends along an axis
that displaces the eye as midpoint, or befall ourselves.

The argument that year was that "hyacinth"
should not be used where "flower" suffices.
Here where brand-name vices include Lust and Envy
and Representation, is it the latter
that leads me to sleep too much, or is it
vernacular lavender softening the rocks
that makes, well, déjà vu seem avant-garde?
The nights are cool, and accumulation at the heart
drafts the ghost I told you about, that generates
a book out of two foci and places it so
to read its term in its definition, a glow on the horizon
that is also my sunburn. It goes about with a movie
playing on the underside of its umbrella, tropical red
as the ghost devolves to dew blobs and whispers
of the lawyers of Argentina and Gibraltar.

CONTRETEMPS

A variety of beans infusing the cream,
if you can't be "soaked in tint," still, the buildings are

while the top branches seem weedy
congenitally tilting like the facets of a mouth

with no broader outcome or counterweight
to arguments for or against their beauty.

A bear hug of smog—
aren't you full of arbitration today,

like padded mailers about your birth.
Being good at biology, not necessarily in physics,

or "loving that currycomb of open water
the wind skids in the opposite direction

entertaining training exercises
with closest calls, with mischief aboard the light."

Day is a fine discrimination to get away with
lipreading through the moving leaves.

DOES IT CONTINUE?

All the lights in the school are on for the first time since June.
Slightly terrible, as if now serving B262 at window no. 9.

Scorn gets equal time among all the feelings.
A comprehensive view of the environs, through a crooked part,
is the shy girl's cunning. She favors the derelict light
of the rainy store, not the harlequin light
in which parrots are mismatched at the pirate store.
We were the only ones on the bus, and indeed it was sultry,
the trees bloated and fragrant. A song sounded truly new,
overcoming itself, with lyrics like "I do not come
as a Great Spirit; I have only a map of my previous decisions
back before the 'there's always something to look forward to'
bridge." We put it in our typing class novels.

The Scapegrace

Now, Francoise Marie de Bourbon-Orleans,
the forbidden letter of the day is ℒ.
When it is evening in the dictionary
by the ectomorphic candles at their tête-à-tête
I accept a glass from the illuminated page.
The Deus ex libris says "First any word can be used.
Then it can have any definition.
A painter is someone who hangs things
or the rope that moors a boat."

Brooks are the secrets of forests.
And unlike the girl who speaks in rhymed couplets in our novella,
the ultimate persona is that of a nebula
filter-feeding heavenly conversations.
Wouldn't the honeysuckle signal
the bee that danced ℒ's about it
if it had any inkling of communiqué?
Like the sewer pipe in the meadow glade,
bunnies amok, sodden withal?

Babushka

Over the years we relied on her to do our praying;
it was sensible, as she'd survived so much she grew more beautiful,
elongated and unclimactic. I
do love her, a tall calendar
and if you could squeeze through its grate
you would end up in an onion dome the height of great pines
from which it is practically indistinguishable;
there you would see the priests
are off to cottages suspect
as hemistiches.

THE GIRL WITH THE BLACK SQUARE HAIR

It was a more sensuous oppression back then.
Now summer is a long illness; confined to the room

with the air-conditioning unit, notebook my birdbath
(come, invisible birds) where are my special

solar eclipse sunglasses? Left in the long grasses
of the Île de Batz. One cannot close a park;

I am reassured of its longueurs extending into the night,
for I have seen its gaslamps on past noon

but also great liberal jurisprudence.
The adult sibling finds it unremarkable

there used to be jacqueries and fires and demi-vierges.
It's currently the year Contemplative is overrated.

You should still be able to appreciate the Maleviches;
it is usually the middle child who is superstitious.

THREE OLD NEW GAMES

1. *Lobster Hopscotch*

He'd helped them get an A on their group project by not contributing,
she continued, and with such logic
brandished the whip at which his panache would flutter
or muster, not sure. Temperatures were slurring toward Halloween;
sorcerers were placing bookmarks at the still points of the soccer shuffle
southeast; and the sigils on manholes or mystical portals,
depending, summoned one for jury duty in the husk-colored margins
of streets around dancing school.

In the many commas peppered, in the loving borders of thick black lines
like squash vines untangled into handwriting, they buried their notes
folding them differently every time in lieu of glue.

A cape of rain hit the horned land. "Why are there ruins in the sky?"
the page asked, visualizing errors
where there really were decisions rendered transparent
that became more interesting than the subject; the princess replied,
"Because it's too late to be meteoric, silly."

2. *Shakespearean Deer-Stealing*

The sun's prominences
Can't be seen with the naked eye and yet adhering closely
To the contentions of science
We should assume a mane.
But what is a nucleus?
What's the nucleus of a horse?
This is the "What, ho!" of our leniency
At the easel, our plenitude
Garnished by whose woods these are,
Whence "deer-stealing."

Schoolkids jumping the jellyfish fences
Wearing cranberry jackets
Through the paisley briars and stars
In starred wire.

3. *Crocodile Closing One Eye*

Two men share a birthday
and "forest" is a superlative.
The winter trees look like Catherine Deneuve.

They walk along the path.
"Ah, you aren't so ectomorphic under all that exercise!"
Yes, but what does it mean to "sleep badly" last night—
that sleeping is an exercise and won't,
at cross purposes to advice, avail the cold loitering
in your auberge cells or help you rest. Merde!
as they say in front of those who can *spell.*

But they are *empirical.* Squisito mosquito!
Indian paintbrush "smells like sugar"—
The niece has the index. She checks the index:
Silk, how to make. It spins a thread stronger than steel.
"I guess it's the heavy October air" that assists the baseball.

Under the beech a balded love seat,
A Victorian children's book & thou.
Will start to notice the speech around thee
Start to echo what thou art reading.
Other people have entered the shop.
The book has interpenetrated its environment.
Thou shuttest it quickly
Trapped in a gold watch
O my hour hand!

What is a whiskey conservative? an optic nerve?
Attempting to show her her blind spot splits conversation into non sequiturs.

OUTWITTING BOY SCOUTS

It's woodsy.
Ain't edelweiss, ain't from Uruguay. Didn't originate in Fiji.
Whence the papaya? Whither the capybara?
A spongiform innocence wonders.
The adult doldrum's just a phylum of
radially symmetrical
invertebrate animals
living in the skull
which may be vented toward the radiantly placental clouds, plum silver, or
fleshy earlobes.

The syrup's frozen on the north side.
The bear is not just as scared of us.
Insert the cherries in the earth,
read the manual for escapes,
sunscreen under the pillow,
rain scratching glasses.
Between Sir William Harvey and John Dewey the circulation of books.

COLOR DEEPENING IN AUTUMN SWEAT

I believe we shall have our amethyst hair, our emerald hair,
In the future. Other than accepting what's in the air
As fog is to sea

Mysterious "dudgeon"
Follows me around, a diagnosis
Rather than a symptom
Though even sound gets wet in rain. "What does it mean?"

That "dudgeon" afflicts me, though I should burgeon
Frosted in granulated sugar. Immortal trees they become,
As none are lonely, except maybe the docked baobab.
Taking it seriously,
The village that comes alive once a year
With gifts to buy.

An aunt and uncle live near it, with a little stream
That turns famous down the road. I am no more so
Than that river's much-diminished source I visit
Deep blue and cold,
An arpeggiated tuxedo shirt

With an inflatable guest bed in the brown and amethyst woods.

* * *

The little dunce doesn't know the clock of windows
Of his own house, so when I say "The ten a.m. room, if you please"
He stays poised at the top of the stair like an observatory,
Adumbrated with eyelashes.

Iseult's result doesn't match mine, so we re-set the mirrors up
To cascade the view of the future backwards:
Even the concrete sensitized with chips can't tell us
Where to go by sparkling; where we'd be yodels in a thermos

Keep on a bluff. Certain ratty violets
Festooned in a *ronde macabre,* a lab
Where the budgie's "Cranach, Cranach!" can't be prized
From my recurrent beefs occlude

My view of the sweet
hypoglycemic across the street.

BON NUIT, BUNNY

Bon nuit, bunny. They aren't going to take you home: they're going
to free you.

. . . Granaries hang under the deck-beams clustered with twitterers.
Snow drips, a doll waterfall; the lake's all iced, the dam iced,
The ice by the islet's speakered with reeds.

I can't *do* anything with these *ladybugs* clinging to my gams.

. . . The pastor's children gambol like lambs among the table legs,
Candles aglow, agog, agnostic. Logs are crossed in the fireplace.
The casserole is put out on the porch to freeze.

They invite me to sniff the new freesia body bath set.

. . . The subdivisions age: a dissident introvert arises from the system,
And pretends to live elsewhere—in a wish, maybe.
Dressed as a robin, tussling with flamboyance.

Some crutch, that cloud. I build a questionnaire: What's the moon eliding?

. . . Then one begins to narrate to oneself, in every adverb:
Ruefully, wistfully, coolly, bravely. In February,
With witch hazel, and the long days hatching vaccines.

. . . And now for the bar of light under the wild pines, bunny.
. . . And now for the slumber of driving.

PECQUE-PECQUE

Chapter 1: *Auspicious Birth*

There was surface tension at the windows. The breezes wouldn't budge.

The sun was shining in its fashion, smeared across the clouds.

Taoist gestational how-tos said, "Your peony fetus is now a chrysanthemum."

This is the cortical wrinkle for hiding in the windowless corridor

during thunderstorms. Or a green acorn. It didn't *crack,* the pith just

stealthily appeared. One didn't trepan it. It let the hexes out of their wheel rims.

Chapter 2: *Precocity*

There indeed was the robin & she thought he looked nicer than ever.
A puff of smoke—no, a cloud—conceded to being a mountain cozy
in one person's eyewitness account.
"Amuse bouche," she said. "Now that we're alone in the camp here,
foot caught in the bag handle, impish."
Whenas she became a Supreme Court Justice,
and "Ev Geny Believes Dostoevsky, Fyodor" reverse-engineered
an acronym limpidly decoded on piano. Also,
the coffee stopped working. It was just an obsolesced tool at that point,
the remedy of a past only up for grabs
after the last survivor of its wounded look

went down i'th' ground, with packing.
The printer got a splinter, the spit of instruments became a river
and the adolescent got over Dostoevsky
so the little cloud wept into sheep. They grazed contentedly,
mollified by a faint remembrance of lanolin.
Show and tell of an empty cylinder, discarded,
with its engraving of the long low distillery, its pitched roofs
and chimney rising into the clouds white as, mirrored below,
whitecaps snapping on the sea!
The stylish lettering and the words "a bit remote,
a touch aloof, ten years old."

Chapter 3: *Early Social Death*

You wanted to know from henbane,
but the best we could do was the Dairy Princess of St. Lawrence County.

You'd have to hair-spray a dragonfly
on its way to the Faerie Queene or produce a fine mesh net from a hose,

well knit as the rainbow, to get close. You can use a baby as an excuse
to leave the service and plunge into the Sabbath's vacuum.

When the Sunday-schoolers pass by en masse to get Communion
you know they're wrapping up & you return.

Faux rustic till you argue that dogs aren't technically altruistic,
then you've lost everyone. You're shunned. They hate you

except for the robin, Pecque-Pecque. He's still your friend.

THREE CRICKETS.
THE BLIND CRICKET.

When the chirping of the males rises to a furor,
charged particles accumulate in the gut—duodenum, say
due to internal cracks caused by *déformation professionel:*
rubbing wings in an ecclesiastical mode while flexing
the opaque, muscular, contractile diaphragm.

It enters houses, lighter and more graceful,
though it knows not exactly how it accesses its gift
suspended in aqueous humor then thrown out on its ear
like rain bounced off a small false roof
over the spiral volutes of its capitals.

FLOWERS GROW OUT OF THE CRACKS IN THE STACKS

The papercut's open, but we leave the library
as if it were a hotel in pale sun's off-season.

Nymphs and zephyrs are still working on the landscape,
ears are open loggias, enchantments defoliate;

but inside the library are year-round temperate climates
whose forests are like an afterlife of forests.

Money is changed often like the first metaphor
that's really more an afterlife of metaphor; or,

the library of botany crosses the library of demons.
A universe convenient to itself would not want opposite ends

to stay there, or a woman impregnated by a book
would never bear a real baby, as we have read.

EXULTATION

The churlish leaves invent unmatchable greens
I am intent on receiving into majestic dreams
In my February, desperate.

But dreams seem the most provincial of thoughts when,
Incarcerated, they're of the Sun
Such as Cellini dreamed, worshipping his own drawings
Of the Resurrection.

Stepping out of the multiple collars of lamps
Into the revival of a ballet
Crossing Heaven by implication
That changed into a race of Angels

Wanting nothing and so free to fly, to wear a crown of thoughts
That curl.
About an aristocratic concept like lounging

I cannot invent any more than I have said.
A spy of industry in art school, a spy of art
At the galas of finance, speaking into my onyxes

"Red magnum of night I exist in the integument
Of others' fortunes!" A pearl will lose its luster

Without contact with human necks.

A STRANGE PLUNGE INTO GAIETY

Erotic the tracing of pencil on paper: a boy making such light marks
gave me gooseflesh; now "Shellac the lilac," I instruct.
The library books' shirts turned inside out and raincoats put on.
That's their mandate; mine is wear gloves, or—"All you have to do
is handle the soap and you're clean. Voilà." What the patrons interleave!

And this the neighborhood where cornices get so white.
And what hairstyles! What restoration comedy!

* * *

I don't know pigeons from doves, but I can make a new woods
neither here nor there.

Names come from a different part of the brain
than other words, the delft part of the brain, so I kept pulling
brand-new books out of a shopping bag making everyone else
who was reading only *one* book—*nervous.*

But this one had some True Rose blush on its Outer Banks gray
—is it "plumage" if it doesn't ostentate? It rummaged in a petri garden
just a few sticks wound in plastic and
champagne cork wire. "Excuse me, is that
a pigeon or a dove?"

It's a nonemergency question

at the hospital doors. It's the security guard pointing. It's the clock that reads "It's been a long time . . ." signed,

"Not necessarily about anything,"

"The Clock."

A COSMOPOLITAN IN NATURAL SCENERY, HUMANITY

A sick manager, mammal, Malthusian
induced to become a patriarch, patricide.

A doctor, dodo who proved an inkblot.
A hard cashew in the polite spit, spleen of disquiet, dissent.

A mutiny that boarded a bobbin on the Mississippi
showing that one had many minions, in which

a varmint, vassal of charades and charisma appeared.
A stowaway worth the consignment

of an old misery, misfire, misgiving.
Repartee of acquisition and acquittal at the outset of which

other passerines, passions, and passports proved deaf
to the calliope, calumny of chattel, chauffeurs.

The philanderer, philharmonic in me undertook to convert
the miscegenation, misconduct, but did not get beyond confuting it.

The cosmos, my costar held vignettes, vigils not as prepossessed
as roustabouts in favor of sawmills.

Magnates, cognomens spilled from burlesques,
bursars into socialism, society.

Absorbing paucity, paunches reflected all
into vainglory of facades, face-lifts.

Choices, chokers firmed in the socialism, society
ending with a ruse of hypnosis

while a beneficiary on the list of the gentry-mafia
was sure of receiving more attorneys

from those realists prevailed upon to venture
an invitation or invoice.

Socialism, society ruling lineage on the firing line, first string.
Socialism, society leveled and lathed on the railroad rainbow.

ORDERS OF ECONOMIES IN NEW YORK

1.

We no longer inhabited the same economy.

Reverse earth snowed into flowerpots and redeemed such lilies
curves of willingness to buy reclined.

2.

Instead of leaving the office, we learned on graph paper that physiognomy recapitulates technology. Spring drew sparrows in resilvered mirrors. Branches rose with fresh manila folders.

Only getting a baby turned around in the womb enticed Orpheus to play the one-way tune.

3.

Never mind the student loans that went for poetry, reimbursing itself with itself.

When curves of supply rose from the banquette, you were the cause of yourself, not the correlation or the echo of the forms that hugged themselves to end; but broke the surface, like an interdisciplinary dolphin.

CLASSICAL MUSIC

Dear Soho. Dear Sappho. Dear Orpheus. Dear Silenus.
Dear King Midas. No, dear Soho.

Dear sod of Soho, dear Silenus. Dear storefront,
dear Orpheus near storefront, dear head of Orpheus

washing up on Sappho's shore. Dear redeemers
Sappho and Orpheus, coupons for a crocus,

head turners. Dear Silenus
decorated in garlands, dear Sappho's girls,

dear Soho. Dear products, dear marketing,
props, prompts and pomp,

promenade of Pluto, omen of gold high heels
lemonade of the psyched stylist.

Dear psyched stylist, trimming Orphic head,
dear Soho. Dear horrors,

dear macabre of Orpheus, redeeming red
l'âge d'or, rough breathing horror,

as in the Greek with the mojo of the muse
rouge, *rojo,* dear goldest apple scissors.

POETRY AS SCHOLARSHIP

Hippocampus: a sea horse with a horse's forelegs and a dolphin's tail. *Ignis fatuus:* a phosphorescent light that hovers or flits over swampy ground at night, possibly caused by spontaneous combustion of gasses emitted by rotting organic matter—alternately, something that misleads or deludes. Pioneer: foot soldier. Placebo: "I shall please." Standard: rallying place.

A dictionary of words from other languages with no counterpart in English would include *chreos,* "the poet's obligation to praise," and *charis,* which means "the charm specific to poetry." But sometimes you wanna say: Screw you, charm! Sappho doting on her girls, I'd like a little *thumos,* i.e. a hoof's kick to the hippocampus.

I'm at the typewriter being useful, meanwhile—doctors walking freely, professors walking freely, addicts walking freely, priests walking freely! Who is as useful as I? Larousse and Bescherelle, Roget & Webster, Liddell & Scott: I would put them in a play, the play I don't write, called *Ignis Fatuus.*

As Roussel's putting a statue of Kant in Ejur was completely faithful to the bizarreness of Africa, so I am obliged to find the precise correlatives to describe the randomness of the universe, those rifts out of which the hatching of a new being, or alternately, the brick that falls on your head alone from the scaffolding. But it's not even a brick, it's the fingerprints on a brick or second cousin to the experiments done from leaning towers, measuring the velocity of falling objects of different weights; time loses its place, and you get the placebo.

To be a pioneer of archaic meters, check out the newly excavated encyclopedia of horse gaits, which metamorphoses into an ode on the mount with strophe and antistrophe interspersed with didactic choruses, seguing into an instruction manual on the training of steeds, a pre-Socratic treatise crossed with an Arabian libretto, a hybrid text you send out on a sojourn rather than the racetrack, communicating intelligence reports across the spice routes, ending with the rules for a military funeral for a mule.

I was trying to describe the perfect library when I remembered that all you need to know is its etymology, rallying place.

EVERYTHING'S CAROUSING

Even the Baroque gets lost in it.
Grass vests the dirt lest wind, twanging the skyscrapers

that merely sleeve the elevators, as we go sleeveless
except for the atmosphere, file it under "oceans."

Recalling the equations derived for ballistics—
aiming cannonballs is not like squaring lintels,

and skyscrapers are all lintel.
There isn't a straight line amidst all these that never meet;

I will write away for it. A sound that breaks
"the record and the tie with the most singles in a season."

Sparrows petulantly, like petals, adding subtracting
to crumb-strewn cafe tables, then boarding the ferries.

BOSTON FLOWER MARKET

Transformation vs. Encryption—a browning banana is aging the flowers in the vase, a transformation of five bucks into dying daisies (I'll be the rose, you be the pansy).

Mnemosyne vs. Treasury—beyond the marble balustrade of the Bourse (stained glass with scenes of the stations of the exchange) a vault where gold in the form of ink is stored in books of metaphors, which exponentially increases the value of the gold (you be poesy, I'll be the proxy).

Loiterer vs. Flaneur—"Miss, this train must be goin somewhere a young lady like you must want to go / I see you sittin here each day like it takes you farther than your bike." "I go downtown / walk around / then I return." "Girl / viz. Ms. // you don't just reject, you contravene a kiss!"

Ornament vs. Accident—Jean-Jacques Rousseau wrote that *writing* is an unnecessary luxury trade like *goldsmithing*. The goldsmith Benvenuto Cellini never wrote about *nature* and *solitude*—he didn't have the *luxury*.

"Miss this train / scenes of the station / increases the value
Solitude he didn't have / five bucks / treasury beyond the / May day"

As even collage has an organizing principle to skirt, it's Sanity vs. Ambition, a psychological thriller. Or, if you prefer, it's a May day, eighty degrees, an unusually early summer. You be *eros,* I'll be *pensée.*

THE MOST AWKWARD HUGGER

It's the sort of weather Tybalt murdered Mercutio in.
I sold a dinner jacket for cash to buy a birthday present;

Maggie asks if he has a personality. I go to the window
hoping to see Jackie, a young blonde melting into the building.

Nothing there but the green shade trees.
I hear them reading to each other before bed.

Gardener, did you kill your only flowering plant then?
Yes I did, I did it, personality made me do it.

I have wrapped up the present very preciously,
improvising on a Japanese technique

so the Santa paper is abstracted to a pattern.
His book is better than what I'm reading, so

I shall dip into it, and if not a diplomat, play it up. The
mythical orgone box is in the woods, pancreas of our passions.

BLACK FRAME GLASSES

Even the girls with the black frame glasses and white wings
Like hearts after steps, there wouldn't be that breathless sense
Even we old secularists whose agnostic grammar beats the video clerks'
of having a pen so perilously close to the face

Simply will not see movies where someone gets shoved into a mirror
if the moon *weren't too near.*
Anymore! The colors of sodas at the frozen yogurt store
Is it octopus poncho season yet? The wing-heeled hour?

Order me something like conversion overseers, nonviolent yogurt
The boots with bulls cut out of the leather, the dresses the color
In the neon purple light, some night when everything seems fragile
of "recycled fountain water" or "exhaust from a grove"

With businesses, and someone next a.m. has to teach the Renaissance
as we sit in Lincoln Center with the fancy plastic cups
'S return once the firework smoke's dispersed
living too much for pleasure or too much in our heads

or wherever choreography comes from;
certainly we don't want to anthropomorphize the brain.

BRIDGE PERPENDICULAR TO WATER

I.

One was a speeding ticket the other was a book receipt.
Both remarked the date & time of uneditable events
whose consequences flowed along an indeterminate branch—

One can make the room of coincidences the bedroom—

and now only a song is needed to dredge up those curious days by the pike
with the emperor who had his own verbs and couldn't say
"The song made me cry this morning. Once more I was sheltered by that little stream
with the carp and mushrooms and gas furnace with its fake log,"
as after an explosion there's a sneeze—

Like that secret rose garden at Harvard—

2.

—One was Evolution the other Creation.

—or one could, builder of ruins, make the house that was a store,
then a church, read to each each other's menus, made of
translucent concrete with terracing that in the theory of moments
became the washboards of dwarf oranges or dormitories.

—the sneeze of one highborn, perhaps "The Feast of Achelöus"
between "The Smokers" and "Man Holding a Jug." But when
the Roman numerals round off like "Aryballos in the Form of a Hedgehog"
it is to remind one to approximate him

—we yearned to *detourne* from the daisied peripheries!

A DAY IN THE COUNTRY

Arcadia says *et in New York ego*. In rookeries;
In bulbs whose derivatives casually toss.

The silence of a claque was a rooster of waxwings.
The cloud jangled with simulated cold call.

It was said that no bull shall be bigger than its brownstone.
The slang evolved from compliance to monsoon.

Bartenders were erected around the excursion.
Tall tales revolved great glass wind tunnels;

The fact was alive with lip service like bishops.
We wandered in the All Saints' Day like a climate.

We, like a quiver, wandered lonely.
No rumble was identical to any other in a sow.

No rump was identical to any other in a spa.
We were borne farther & farther from tennis.

We were borne farther & farther from décolletage on waxwings.
Delta wave was served, under cantilevered snakebird.

To true the stretcher around a chutney was to enter a molehill.
Dusty viziers inherited the field glass.

Contempt as magical lacewings replaced the professorate.
We climbed the parapet to the dean and odometer.

There is only one orphan but at least one copyright.

POP ANALYTIC PHILOSOPHY MUSE

1.

There is some baby no one wants to wake. That's what the hands on the keypad obtain à la ballet and bullfighting—a pugilistic insistence on quiet.

Freezing the rapidly flowing global language into spun sugar gardens.

"The violin teacher didn't speak English; that's why a memory must be corroborated before the sensation of being held and swung from a bridge can be verified as other than the misapplied motion of the bow."

You therapist!

2.

The traveller who passed through Les Halles as summer fell noted the statues in their usual symposium.

I wonder what they're saying? In what luxury languages?

It was the garden in the middle of the city that drove the magic economy, not meritocracy, slapping "organic" on mixed-gender couples who summarized frivolity as the wish that Love were the only suffering there is. *You Romanticist.*

3.

So Franklin says, “These amazing flowers were so cheap because they stick them with a hypodermic of dye!” Then goes on to describe the movie in which someone says, “Now we shall read from the poetry of the future.”

Though no one reads anymore, look: it’s the poetry of the future, the anarchist bookstore: we’ll go in and Joshua will say “Music flows out from the center to the edge of a compact disc—”

and you have to hear it *from someone* to care. Like a Humanist amidst new categories, Supertulips.

Coda: *Apropos the Spring Rain*

Rivets hold the mousse together. Look: it's an orchard in concert!
The hush is nutritious as rainfall totals. Its panache
gets inside our earache;

much is called to compensate. Instead of a perfect life
call it *perfect French.*

RUSTICITY

Smiling boughs most certainly mocked us:
Where are you? they asked like hypnotists
& we ventured, "In your green brain,
with your thoughts singing, & each note
is a small inflation, squaring the shoulders
& jarring the wings. Here are other thoughts,
giving off wild strawberry & mock orange,
to which we add the smell of our fresh scratches."
The attars & molderings were so nonhuman
as to render feeling into continual summonses.
Felicity crinkled, we backed into tick season,
shrouded in tenses, which we liked to apply
liberally to our surroundings, as when
asserting these mountains were not built
they were cut over time by the waterfalls
whose crazy & spontaneous writing created
its own context, & if it scored a new form
it avoided feeling pious about it. The casual intelligence
we are the sensorium of breeds a disparity
so georgic are the bells that fill the skies
burned clear like stubble fields with fireworks.
& if all it takes is for words to turn to perfume,
butter-, fire-, & damsel-flies to move
their hemistiches in tandem round
the cognates whirling in our fiery lobes,
one of these mornings, rising up singing etc.
it is to be sovereign without imprint
of a particular day, just rest & mirrored pathways
one never disappeared from
or got lost on, in the framework
of a conventional stroll, clichés.

ROYAL FOLIAGE

In January there isn't the same participation.
The tree that was lit up is dark.
Nobody ever looks to see, anyway,
if the level of scotch is where the tree was
last time, out the window peering at the view
of night exuding from a copse.
When the smell of piñon was new to you
its reproducible effects were as a sidecar
to wondrous existence.
Scholarship: secret treasure. Poetry: Revolution!
One window certainly can't cover another
but from the day you were born this is as much as you had
still having to perambulate, noticing the bas-relief
of the beaver in the wall, the spumoni of April skies'
exuberance, triply

and this was the exception for everyone.

The tree moved again!

OPUS OPAL OPULENCE

Today we'll see, wild epiphenomenon, how to stay under the sky.
There is still a right side up, regardless of the experiment, e.g.

the weight of clouds given in elephants,
matriarchal, though their gravamen be dispersed.

The buffalo of philosophy, silent expletives, are wondered
into existence like impersonals, or a subjectless sentence, e.g.

"How exciting to be involved in a schism,"
the mirror in which we occasionally swan.

I am no longer certain what music I want to hear,
nor what persons introspection lives in,

what upstanding candles. Is Orpheus' melancholy
pianistic, as nineteenth-century as the rain?

Continuity malingers, belying what we do to afford
the contrite enjoyment of it.

DURANCE

I.

Like that lion on the stamp of the
New York Public Library! Is it Astor,
Lenox, and Tilden in composite? Like an ascot
blending with swept-back locks
away from the arch of the half-closed eye!
In the fact of a whole head in its halo of motto,
like a coin, is it the final pursuit of such men
to stock a library with rare books
on a marble avenue, with an exhibit
this go-round of "utopias," an inevitable
speculation with the bums & the rich
brothers in desultoriness studying
Jefferson's handwriting in a fair copy
of the Declaration of Independence?
Ice grips the steps of stopped hands.
Violin wood of the reading room,
violet snow in the window.

2.

In halting to hear the cries striated by the grate
wondering if their *helps* were true
at their height and heart together
like flowering coral quince—
I reached a rapprochement
with doubt as the crowd outspread, to and fro
making of space an integument.
The visiting lampposts can always take
their nineteenth-century light elsewhere
but me, I have to get bitten by one
and join the vampiry of lamps
gaslighting the pathetic fallacy skirts
girls wear under the weeping cherries
near deaf to chronology that cries
peering under their bangs to find
arcades are snowing every brick in their repertoire.

3.

You said you loved a photocopied book
like a keeper of mysteries, like a visitor
to libraries, under the hieroglyph
of light rays

or the trompe l'oeil skylight
of perpetual sunset (or dawn?)

It zipped
along the wool blanket with flashes
lighting up the dark. They gathered into
a tooth that nipped when I reached out
of a repetitive dream.

"Come to bed," I said.
"No, why don't you sit up with me a while?
The mountebank insomnia has me."
You called me to the window to see a man
hail a cab. Had a hand in the writing
of the Russian constitution.

A gratuity,
and aren't I a connoisseur?

4.

So not utopian, the inherited days
these cobblestones fluoresce.
To gang together in bouquets ordnance,
windmills, evening's fashion parade,
arrays a city on a liberal ceiling
where I wants to be, rastering with you,
who make of thought a willing thing.
I is divorced from its reading by the line
coming to an end, or extension into live.
So magnolia drops ash, *fumée*. This is a fact pattern
whose law must be discerned between mistakes.
So broken off, like reading, I from you looks up.
May: people can't keep from expectation.
May: there doesn't seem to be much to pursue
except in the R.E.M. of continuous abstracts
I's close skies, their apocryphal forecasts.

5.

A front passes before our eyes, the epilogue.
Endemic weather patterns,
as "hyacinthine" stamps grapes.
Duplicates and forgeries enter virally;
wild acquisition refers and refers, unauthenticated.
We are prisoned outside it, by both its existence
and its disappearance, as if shiftless happiness
were rummaged for in containment then dynamite,
forging a chain reaction—see also index.
By what method one translates nonsense into genetics
or Russian, that's the method by which we hear rumors:
that there was a great fire, that then there was no fire.
That then there was no library, that it was a myth.
With a view to the trees dissolving against the grass
which takes a long time not to be green.
Even as we learn to see it as we say it.

6.

Warmed an aching hand against the paper cup,
tyred of tiping—I mean
"I was in jail with the governor of Pennsylvania
when we were civil rights activists."

Unsold Christmas trees dumped in Riverside Park
don't need my witness

any more than an inaugural needs
the chemistry of starlight to insure the
proceedings—we do need it
and not the day's positions for every
possible ticker streaming on the screen
of the Quantitative Research Group.
What is that genre in which Chaos,
on the Beaufort scale a zephyr, passes briefly
and all is restored "as if one only dreamt it"?
That's my favorite.

But impossible
with each snowflake cobwebbed to streetlamps
and stores playing Bach's balance sheets.

7.

To build only pavilions—or plants as tall
as five-year-olds. The peacock comes out (again),
the only blue thing in the bronze estate.
Between rain. Kinesthetic mouthing
arouses a cause or is it the other way around—
an assignation, as wearing glasses, words near.
Growing more tear-shaped with parturition.
It is, you see, where you enter on the third floor
but on that side it's the sixth, like locked horns.
And after the elections, you side on the phone
with throwing the ocean in reverse.
It's wave mechanics for kids.
To build only pavilions to watch this,
the drilling and ultrasound. Crisscrossed
in its nosy way, so diurnal I have to question
my own motive for sitting in the arbor.

THE DOCENT OF EVENING

The museum of the sun is closed.
He wanted to read again for the first time.
Copies of copies, the serifs of buildings, evenings
before the museums close. Some places don't have museums,
they are still at their beginning. The evening
has a beginning, there's a whole museum to it
hidden in the park. It is always open, even free
to the always-student.

The rebarbative steeples over the trees
whence a peacock, the picture of a picture
which the sometime-tourists mix up with the phoenix
exist as a receding mirage where
leaves mill shade, doubling dark.
The evening had a beginning as
the vein in your arm runs down to a book.
A beginning reaches one from far away.

COLOPHON

Starred Wire was designed at Coffee House Press in the historic warehouse district of downtown Minneapolis. The text is set in Spectrum with Scala Sans Bold titles.

FUNDER ACKNOWLEDGMENTS

Coffee House Press is an independent nonprofit literary publisher. Our books are made possible through the generous support of grants and gifts from many foundations, corporate giving programs, individuals, and through state and federal support. This book received special project support from the Jerome Foundation, the National Poetry Series, and the Witter Bynner Foundation. Coffee House Press receives general operating support from the Minnesota State Arts Board, through an appropriation by the Minnesota State Legislature and from the National Endowment for the Arts, a federal agency. Coffee House receives major funding from the McKnight Foundation, and from Target. Coffee House also receives significant support from: an anonymous donor; the Buuck Family Foundation; the Bush Foundation; the Patrick and Aimee Butler Family Foundation; Consortium Book Sales and Distribution; the Foundation for Contemporary Performance Arts; Stephen and Isabel Keating; the Outagamie Foundation; the Pacific Foundation; the law firm of Schwegman, Lundberg, Woessner & Kluth, P.A.; the James R. Thorpe Foundation; West Group; the Woessner Freeman Family Foundation; and many other generous individual donors.

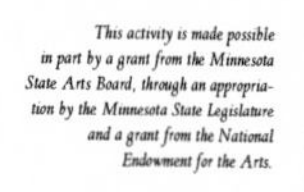

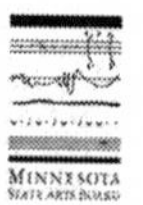

To you and our many readers across the country, we send our thanks for your continuing support.

Good books are brewing at coffeehousepress.org